Crafting Authenticity: Building a Brand with Genuine Identity

Betty T. Vargas

TABLE OF CONTENT

CHAPTER 1

Introduction to Authenticity

What Is Authenticity?

Presenting a real, truthful, and authentic picture of your company is the foundation of authenticity in branding. It entails adhering to your basic principles, being open and honest about your goals and methods, and avoiding exaggerated or deceptive representations. Essentially, the process involves developing a brand identity that accurately represents your company's essence and connects with your target market to build credibility and enduring relationships.

Examining Its Importance:

 Authenticity has a significant impact on customer loyalty, trust, and opinion of a brand overall;

1. Trust-Building: By reassuring customers that a company is sincere in its goals and deeds, authenticity fosters trust. Customers are more likely to trust a brand when they believe it to be honest.

2. Increased Loyalty: Genuine brands have a stronger emotional bond with their clientele. Customers are more likely to stick with a company if they believe it lives up to its promises and is authentic.

3. Positive Brand Perception: A positive brand image is influenced by authenticity. Transparency is something that consumers value in brands, and it has a favorable impact on the brand's perception in the marketplace.

4. Differentiation in the Market: A brand that is authentic stands out from rivals. In a global world where genuineness is highly valued by customers, authenticity turns into a differentiator for a company.

5. Resilience in Adversity: Genuine brands have a tendency to handle adversity better. When a brand has built loyalty and trust via authenticity, people are more understanding when things go hard.

Essentially, the significance of authenticity goes beyond mere trust; it establishes a strong and favorable brand image and builds enduring relationships with customers.

Case Studies:

Numerous companies have adopted authenticity with success, reaping benefits in the process:

1. Patagonia: This genuine brand has made a name for itself by supporting sustainability and environmental problems. Customers that care about the environment have responded well to this pledge, increasing brand loyalty.

2. Dove: Dove promoted honesty and self-acceptance through their "Real Beauty" campaign, which questioned conventional notions of beauty. This strategy improved the brand's relationship with a variety of audiences in addition to receiving great praise.

3. TOMS: TOMS is a prime example of a company dedicated to social responsibility. Their "One for One" business model offers a pair of shoes for each pair sold. This genuine approach has produced great word-of-mouth marketing in addition to aiding in the brand's development.

4. Airbnb: By highlighting distinctive, regional experiences, Airbnb has promoted authenticity.Airbnb has established a brand that is synonymous with genuine connections between hosts and guests, as well as meaningful travel experiences.

5. Warby Parker: By providing reasonably priced, fashionable glasses and an open supply chain, Warby Parker upended the eyeglass market. This sincerity has drawn clients seeking out true value and moral business conduct.

These illustrations show how incorporating authenticity into a company's identity and operations may boost customer loyalty and trust while also producing favorable brand results.

Obstacles & Difficulties

It can be difficult to maintain authenticity in branding, so it's important to be aware of potential dangers. The following are some obstacles and methods to get beyond them:

1. Claims of Inauthenticity and Greenwashing:
   - Challenge: A brand's credibility might be harmed by claims of greenwashing or insincerity.
   - Strategy: Communicate sincere pledges, maintain transparency in sustainability initiatives, and support assertions with quantifiable actions.

2. Scale and Consistency: - Challenge: As a brand expands, it gets harder to stay true to itself at different touch points.
   - Approach: Create precise brand standards, teach staff members about fundamental principles, and periodically check for brand coherence.

3. Shifting Expectations of Consumers:
   - Challenge: As consumer expectations change, brands may find it difficult to truly adapt.
   - Approach: Keep a watchful eye on market developments, aggressively solicit input, and be flexible in adapting tactics to suit changing conditions.
4. Corporate Scandals:
- Problem: A brand's validity might be damaged by scandals or disputes.
   - Approach: Be open about problems, accept accountability, and show that you're doing something to make things right and stop this kind of thing from happening again.

5. Balancing Commercial Interests:
- Challenge: Genuine brand practices may conflict with financial aims.
- Strategy: Integrate authenticity into company plans to align commercial objectives with brand values, and prioritize long-term reputation over short-term advantages.

Brands may avoid potential problems and preserve authenticity by proactively addressing these issues, which will guarantee a long-lasting and fruitful relationship with their audience.

Examining Its Importance:

Authenticity and essential brand principles must be emphasized in order to establish a true brand identity. This includes:

1. Defining Core Values: Outlining the essential ideas that direct the decisions and activities of the brand in a clear and concise manner.

2.Maintaining Consistency: Coordinating these fundamental values with all facets of the brand, from communication to the provision of goods and services.

3. Establishing Trust: By exhibiting a dedication to openness and sincerity, communicating truthfully about the brand's principles establishes trust.

4. Making a Meaningful Connection with the Audience: Authenticity strikes a chord with customers who have similar beliefs, forging a bond that transcends business dealings.

5. Differentiating in the Market: Authenticity turns into a distinctive mark that helps a business stand out from rivals and draw in like-minded clients.

By putting brand values at the center of authenticity, companies not only build a unique identity, but also lay the groundwork for enduring connections with clients who value and share the brand's core values.

The chapter seeks to prepare the reader for understanding the crucial role authenticity plays in developing an engaging and reliable brand by providing this basis.

CHAPTER 2

Unveiling Your Brand Story

Contextual history

Take the following actions to authentically tell the story of how your brand began:

1. Founder Interviews: - Hold in-depth interviews with the founders to learn about their own driving forces, original goals, and early difficulties.

2. Timeline Creation: - Create a timeline that details important choices, occasions, and milestones in the history of the brand.

3. Visual Assets: - Include images that give a concrete link to the brand's origins, such as old photos, early sketches, or any other pertinent artifacts.

4. Emotional Connection: - Highlight the founders' ardor and commitment to the story to bring emotion into the narrative. Give stories that demonstrate their dedication to the brand's objective.

5. Overcoming Challenges: - Clearly state the difficulties encountered in the early going, such as monetary difficulties, doubt about the market, or operational roadblocks. Give an example of the founders' tenacity.

6. Customer Testimonials: - Provide testimonials from brand ardent supporters who were there from the beginning, demonstrating the influence and confidence that the company fostered.

7. Consistency with Brand Values: - Connect the story to the brand's present values by showing how the original inspirations and difficulties still influence the brand's personality.

These components can be used to produce a real and engaging story that not only illustrates the history of the company but also forges strong bonds with your target audience.

Goals and Objectives

To eloquently state the brand's goal and vision and demonstrate how these values inform every facet of the company, use the following actions:

1. Formulate a Well-defined Mission Statement: Create a succinct and powerful mission statement that describes the brand's main objectives, core values, and purpose.

2. Define the Vision: - Clearly state the brand's long-term goals, including the future it hopes to build and the influence it hopes to have on the public or its clients.

3. Alignment with Values: - Showcase how the brand's guiding principles guide decisions and activities by tying the goal and vision to these principles.

4. Integration into Operations: - Provide particular instances of how the goal and vision are incorporated into daily operations, such as customer service and product development.

5. Employee Engagement: - Showcase how staff members share the brand's objective and vision, highlighting their part in making these ideas a reality.

6. Impact on Customer Experience: - Highlight the value that customers receive beyond the products or services and explain how the brand's mission and vision directly influence the customer experience.

Measurable goals should be established in order to show that the brand is committed to actively pursuing and accomplishing its stated purpose. These goals should be in line with the mission and vision.

A brand can guarantee that its vision and mission become essential to the success of the company and act as guiding principles by articulating these elements clearly.

Personal stories

Putting personal tales or experiences that demonstrate the brand's adherence to its principles front and center requires planning and thought:

1.Collect Employee Stories:- Inspire staff members to contribute firsthand accounts that exemplify the principles of the company. This could be accomplished through specialized storytelling sessions, staff newsletters, or internal messaging.

2.Customer Testimonials:- Ask for and display customer testimonials that particularly point out situations in which the brand's values improved their experience. Post these endorsements on your website, in social media posts, or in promotional materials.

3.Founder or Leadership Narratives:- Inquire of the founders or the leadership group why particular ideals are significant to them in light of their individual experiences. Video content, interviews, and blog pieces might all be used for this.

4.Case Studies: - Create comprehensive case studies that explore particular circumstances in which the brand's values played a key role in choices and results. These might be effective instruments for displaying dedication.

5.Visual Storytelling:- Add visual components to these tales, such pictures or movies. Enhancing emotional connections and making events more relatable are two benefits of visual storytelling.

6.Employee Recognition Programs: - Create initiatives that honor and commend staff members that uphold the core principles of the company. Tell their tales both inside and outside the company to provide real-world examples of dedication.

7. Events and Workshops:- Conduct workshops or events that revolve on the core values of the brand. Permit participants to tell their own tales in order to build a collective story that highlights the brand's dedication.

8. Collaborations and Partnerships:- Emphasize experiences from joint ventures or partnerships that reflect the ideals of the brand. This can involve cooperative efforts, neighborhood initiatives, or triumphs that are shared.

9. Interactive Campaigns: - Develop campaigns that are interactive on your website or social media, inviting staff members and customers to share their own narratives that align with the brand's principles.

10. Consistency in message:- Make sure that the stories you offer complement the brand's positioning and overall message. Authenticity is strengthened by consistency.

Through the implementation of these tactics, a brand may successfully showcase individual narratives that embody its values, cultivating a stronger bond with internal and external stakeholders.

Customer Impact
Strategic communication and storytelling are needed to provide real-world instances of how the brand's values have benefited consumers, communities, or the industry. Here's how to make this happen:

1.Acquire Impact Stories: - Continually look for and gather accounts from clients, neighbors, or business associates who have benefited from the brand's principles. You can accomplish this by direct outreach, interviews, or surveys.

2. Case Studies:- Create thorough case studies that illustrate certain situations in which the brand's principles have a noticeable impact. To demonstrate impact, use numerical data, testimonies, and before-and-after situations.

3.Video Testimonials:- Produce powerful video testimonials in which people discuss their experiences and explain how the brand's ideals have improved their lives. Storytelling using images can be quite effective.

4. Highlight Community efforts: - Highlight the brand's participation in charitable endeavors or community efforts that are consistent with its core principles. Tell tales of the beneficial effects these projects have had on the neighborhood.

5.Industry Recognition:- Emphasize any accolades, certificates, or honors the brand has obtained for its dedication to values in the industry. The favorable influence gains legitimacy from this external evaluation.

6.Infographics and Visual Representations: - Create visual aids or infographics that clearly illustrate the significance of the brand's core principles. You can use these images on your website, in presentations, and on social media.

7. Work together with influencers: Join together with thought leaders or influencers in your field who can offer gratifying experiences that align with the principles of your company. Your message may be amplified by their support.

8. Host Events or Webinars: - Plan webinars or events where you talk about and provide actual cases of how your brand's values have had an impact. Invite important parties to share their story, such as clients and locals.

9.Fix Content Frequently:- Keep a part of your blog or website devoted to sharing impact stories. Update this information frequently to maintain the story's vibrancy and reflect the continuous good contributions.

10.Be Active on Social Media:- Use social media channels to post updates, testimonials, or bite-sized tales about how the company's principles are bringing about good change. Invite people to share their experiences with you.

A company may show its audience that it is committed to values by actively and openly sharing these real-world examples, which also encourages audience trust and loyalty.

Evolution Over Time

Simple and efficient actions can be taken to demonstrate adaptation without sacrificing authenticity and communicate how the brand has changed while adhering to its basic values:

1. Write a Narrative: -Create an engaging story that highlights the brand's development while staying true to its guiding principles. The story should detail the brand's journey. This tale should emphasize difficulties, lessons learned, and significant events.

2. Visual Timeline:- Make an infographic or visual timeline that illustrates the brand's development over time. Add noteworthy occurrences, adjustments, or the introduction of new goods or services that demonstrate flexibility while adhering to basic principles.

3. Record Modifications Openly:- Clearly state any adjustments or modifications made to the trademark. Changes in the target market, brand messaging, or product offerings are examples of this. Being transparent is essential to preserving authenticity.

4.Showcase Customer Feedback:- Share encouraging comments from customers that highlight the brand's capacity to change and grow without sacrificing its essential principles. Testimonials from real people can support authenticity.

5.Highlight Innovation: - Draw attention to the ways in which the brand has embraced new technologies or innovated while maintaining its core values. This demonstrates flexibility in a market that is evolving.

6.Employee Stories:- Highlights from staff members who have participated in the development of the brand. Their personal stories can demonstrate the brand's steadfast adherence to principles even in times of transition.

7.Update Brand Messaging Frequently- Make sure your messaging is consistent with your core principles and reflects the most recent advancements. Update your website's content, social media communications, and marketing materials frequently.

8.Interact with Stakeholders:- Take an active interest in interacting with stakeholders, such as partners, employees, and consumers, to learn about their perspectives on the brand's development. Make adjustments to your communication plan based on these comments.

9.Educate About Industry Trends:- Inform your audience about the developments in the industry that have shaped the progress of the brand. Present these modifications as calculated adjustments to maintain relevance while upholding moral principles.

10.Host Behind-the-Scenes Content:- Share behind-the-scenes content to give an authentic peek into how the brand has developed, such as leadership interviews, office tours, or development procedures.

Through the implementation of these measures, a brand may demonstrate adaptability and reaffirm its dedication to key values while communicating its evolution in an effective manner. With the audience, this strategy fosters credibility and trust.

CHAPTER 3

Audience Alignment

1. Define Your Target Audience: - Clearly state the traits, inclinations, and actions of the audience that are consistent with the ideals of your brand.

2.Craft Tailored Messaging:- Create content that speaks directly to and addresses the needs and values of your target audience.

3.Utilize Relevant Channels:- Make sure your brand is visible where your target audience is most likely to interact by selecting communication channels that they frequently use.

4.Participate in Conversations:- Actively join in discussions on issues linked to your brand's beliefs on social media and other platforms.

5.Use Influencers: - Work with people who are similar in values to your brand or influencers. Their support can assist in connecting with a larger audience that values your genuineness.

6.Get and Examine comments:-Solicit and examine audience comments and their answers. Make use of this knowledge to hone your strategy and establish a stronger rapport with their expectations.

7.Showcase Shared Values:- Consistently highlight your brand's values in marketing materials, making sure they coincide with those of your intended audience.

8.Create Interactive Content:- Provide engaging interactive content to build a feeling of community around your brand and to encourage audience participation.

These easy-to-follow guidelines can help you find and engage with customers that truly identify with your real brand, building stronger bonds and promoting brand loyalty.

CHAPTER 4

Designing Genuine Visuals

Developing a visual identity that truly embodies your brand requires careful planning and attention to detail:

1.Define Brand components:- Clearly state the colors, typography, photography, and graphic components that best express your brand. Make sure these complement the personality and values of your brand.

2. Know Your Target Audience:- Take into account the inclinations and sour patches of your intended audience. Design visuals to appeal to people and arouse the feelings you want them to.

3. Create a Distinctive Logo: - Create a logo that captures the soul of your brand. A logo ought to be scalable, memorable, and representative of the essence of your company.

4. Select Appropriate Colors:- Pick a color scheme that communicates the feelings and traits connected to your brand. Make sure all visual elements use the same colors.

5.Typography Selection:- Select fonts that accentuate the character of your brand. In order to preserve a consistent visual identity across various media, take into account scalability and legibility.

6.Create Consistent Imagery: - Compile a collection of photos that complement the messaging and values of your brand. To strengthen authenticity, make sure that the style, tone, and subject matter are all consistent.

7.Design Style requirements:- Clearly define the brand's usage requirements for visual components. Establish guidelines for usage, dimensions, and spacing to preserve a unified brand identity.

8.Integrate Brand Storytelling:- Incorporate your brand's mission and story into visual components. The visual identity's legitimacy may be strengthened by this relationship.

9. Adapt to Different Platforms:- Take into account how your visual identity appears on different platforms to ensure adaptation while keeping a consistent and identifiable brand image.

10. Solicit Feedback:- To make sure that your visual identity is connecting genuinely, gather input from stakeholders, staff members, and even members of the target audience.

By keeping these things in mind when creating your visual identity, you can create a genuine and appealing portrayal of your brand that not only draws in your target market but also effectively conveys the essence and character of your company.

CHAPTER 5

Transparency in Operations

Enhancing authenticity requires integrating openness into company procedures. Here's a thorough breakdown of how to accomplish this:

1.Open Communication:-Encourage candid communication among team members. Encourage open communication between management and staff to foster an atmosphere where knowledge is openly exchanged.

2.Public Disclosure: - Inform the public about pertinent company facts. Financial reports, sustainability programs, or information regarding the sourcing and production procedures could all fall under this category.

3.Ethical Business Practices:- Specify and follow moral business conduct. Show that you are committed to ethical sourcing, conscientious environmental policies, and treating employees fairly.

4.Customer Education:- Inform clients about the procedures that your company uses. Make it clear where materials come from, how things are created, and any ethical issues that are included into your business processes.

5.Clear Policies:- Create and disseminate clear policies about matters like product quality, customer service, and data privacy. Customers are better able to anticipate thanks to this transparency.

6.Event Handling Openness: - When faced with difficulties or emergencies, be open and honest about the state of affairs, the steps you've done, and your plans for resolving them. This candor increases credibility and confidence.

7.Stakeholder Engagement:- Interact with consumers, staff members, and local communities as well as other stakeholders. Ask for their opinions, respond to their worries, and actively include them in the decision-making process.

8.Social Responsibility Reporting:- Disseminate information about your social responsibility efforts on a regular basis. This can entail giving back to the community, getting involved in charities, and making an attempt to have an influence that goes beyond making money.

9.Accessibility of Information:- Provide easy access to information. Use social media, corporate websites, and other means of communication to provide pertinent information about your business procedures.

10.Employee Involvement:- Encourage staff members to contribute their ideas and involve them in decision-making processes. Genuine and positive corporate culture is facilitated by engaged workforce members.

Transparency improves authenticity and fosters trust with internal and external stakeholders when it is included into these areas of your organization. This dedication to transparency creates a real bond with your audience and adds to the overall legitimacy of your company.

CHAPTER 6

Building Trust and Loyalty

Building trust and loyalty is fundamental for a brand's success. Here's a concise guide on achieving this:

1. Consistent Branding:
   - Maintain a consistent and authentic brand image across all touchpoints to reinforce reliability and recognition.

2. Reliable Product/Service Quality:
   - Deliver high-quality products or services consistently to meet or exceed customer expectations.

3.Transparency:
   - Be transparent about your business practices, values, and any challenges you may face. Honesty fosters trust.

4.Customer Engagement:
   - Actively engage with your customers through various channels. Respond to feedback, answer queries, and make them feel heard and valued.

5. Personalized Experiences:

- Tailor experiences to individual customer preferences when possible. Personalization enhances the sense of connection.

6.Exceptional Customer Service:
   - Provide exceptional customer service by being responsive, helpful, and going the extra mile to resolve issues.

7. Consistent Communication:
   - Keep customers informed about updates, promotions, and any changes that might affect their experience with your brand.

8. Social Responsibility:
   - Engage in socially responsible practices. Show commitment to causes that align with your values, resonating positively with customers.

9. Loyalty Programs:
   - Implement loyalty programs that reward repeat customers. This encourages ongoing engagement and strengthens loyalty.

10. Surprise and Delight:
   - Occasionally surprise customers with unexpected perks, discounts, or exclusive access, fostering a sense of appreciation.

11. Community Building:
   - Create a sense of community around your brand. Encourage customers to share their experiences and connect with each other.

12. Consistent Improvement:
   - Continuously strive to improve your products, services, and customer experience based on feedback and changing market dynamics.

By focusing on these elements, a brand can establish a foundation of trust and loyalty, creating a positive relationship with its customer base that goes beyond mere transactions.

CHAPTER 7

Consistency in Communication

Keeping consistency and creating a unified brand image require that your messaging be loyal to your brand's identity across all platforms. Here are some easy methods to make this happen:

1. Create Detailed Brand Guidelines:- Establish thorough brand guidelines that elucidate your brand's identity, encompassing essential message, tone of voice, fundamental values, and visual components. Make sure that everyone in the team has easy access to these guidelines.

2.Train Your Team:- Educate your team members on the brand rules, focusing on marketing, sales, and customer service. Make sure that everyone is aware of how crucial it is to keep communications consistent.

3.Centralized Communication Hub:- Create a document or hub for centralized communication that houses all authorized material, messages, and brand assets. This guarantees that the most recent information is available to all.

4.Regularly evaluate and Update:- To adjust to any changes in your company, market dynamics, or industry trends, regularly evaluate and update your brand standards. Make sure the guidelines are up to date and accurately represent your brand.

5.Cross-Functional Collaboration: - Encourage departmental cooperation to coordinate communications initiatives. Promote candid dialogue and criticism to make sure messaging is consistent with the brand.

6. Use a Content Calendar: - Create a content calendar that lists the messages that will be distributed through different channels. This aids in message scheduling and coordination to guarantee tone and content uniformity.

7.Install Approval Procedures:- Create approval procedures for all communications that are directed toward the outside world. This guarantees that, even before it reaches your audience, messaging is consistent with the identity of your brand.

8. Monitor Social Media and Customer Feedback: - Keep an eye out for any messaging inconsistencies by routinely monitoring social media platforms and customer feedback. Respond to any issues right away and modify the message as necessary.

9. Consistent Visual Branding:- Make sure that visual components, including imagery, color schemes, and logos, are consistent throughout all media. Your brand identification is strengthened by using consistent visual branding.

10. Conduct Periodic Audits: - To find any deviations, periodically audit your communications across all channels. Over time, this proactive strategy aids in preserving uniformity.

You can create a strong structure to guarantee that your messaging is always faithful to your brand's identity across all platforms by putting these steps into practice. Maintaining consistency in your brand's communication with your audience helps to build brand awareness, trust, and overall effectiveness.

CONCLUSION

In conclusion, developing authenticity is essential to creating a brand that has a true identity. As we've discussed, authenticity entails matching your brand's origin narrative, mission, and visual identity to every aspect of it with sincerity and truth. Customers respond well to this sincere approach, which promotes brand loyalty, trust, and favorable perception.

Your brand becomes a true representation of a shared ethos rather than just a collection of goods or services when you embrace transparency in business procedures, share real stories, and operate consistently in accordance with your fundamental principles.

Recall that authenticity requires constant dedication. Remain loyal to your origins and carry on having honest and transparent interactions with your audience as your brand develops. By doing this, your brand will be able to grow over time and become recognized by your target audience as a reliable and genuine presence.